Ma

Author:

Riverhouse Stories

Facebook + Instagram

Friend

Thanks to Carolyn Ogburn

A River Runs Under It

40 Years on a Houseboat in Oregon

Aunt Mattie Books, a Dakota/Oregon imprint

Text Copyright © 2020 Andrea Carlisle
Cover Photo: Andrea Carlisle
Book design: Sarah Klinger
Cover design: Michael Mathers
Paintings: Salli

The photo of Andrea Carlisle and Carson and the photo of Aunt Mattie are by Michael Mathers.
All other photos are by Andrea Carlisle.
The poem "Houseboat" originally appeared in *The Texas Observer*.
For information or to book an event, send request to andrea@andreacarlisle.com.

A CIP record for this book is available from the Library of Congress Cataloging-in-Publication Data

ISBN-13: 978-0-578-68511-3

A River Runs Under It

40 Years on a Houseboat in Oregon

———

ANDREA CARLISLE

For my neighbors—the humans, animals, birds, and fish—who make each day on the river a good day, and for anyone anywhere who has ever called a river home.

We call upon the waters that rim the earth, horizon to horizon, that flow in our rivers and streams, that fall upon our gardens and fields, and we ask that they teach us and show us the way.

— from a Chinook blessing litany

CONTENTS

PART ONE

A Brief History

1972

Following a year of teaching at an international school in Kuwait, I moved to Portland. After life in the desert, my eyes craved every shade of green offered by the Pacific Northwest. I couldn't get enough of the waterfalls and ferny trails of the Columbia River Gorge, couldn't run far enough or fast enough along the beaches and hiking paths of the nearby ocean, or lie long enough in the grass, stoned with friends, under the emerald canopies of city parks.

I'd grown up in a series of small towns across the Midwest, all with woods nearby. The streams and trees of those places had always been my refuge after each unsettling childhood move. The closest thing to the landscape of the Midwest that I'd heard about in my new location was a sparsely populated island just outside the city. I wanted to spend time roaming the flat, open, and wooded spaces Portlanders described, but even after a year in the city, I hadn't yet gotten around to actually going there. Then one day in the fall of 1972, a strange thing happened in close proximity to this place.

I was driving along Highway 30 headed toward the ocean with my five-month-old puppy Carson, a whippet mix, by my side. I hoped to get a glimpse of Sauvie Island on the way. I knew it was off that highway somewhere. I just didn't know exactly where.

Carson sat beside me, attentive and curious about the road, raising her long muzzle now and again to sniff deeply as the smells of the city and industrial district receded behind us and the country opened up. I'd lived in Portland only a short time when she was born in the spring at the communal house I shared with a group of others in our twenties who had recently arrived in the Northwest from elsewhere. She seemed content to occupy the passenger seat, occasionally standing up on her stick-legs, maybe curious as to why we'd driven farther than ever before. I couldn't wait to get us to the Pacific for her first run there.

I'd driven about twenty minutes when I turned my head in her direction. Smitten as I was with this little dog, I could have been turning toward her to admire again those long legs, the pointy delicate muzzle extending out from under the puppy flop of her ears, the amber splashes of color on her white coat reminding me of a pinto pony. But the way I took my eyes from the road and turned my head suddenly to the right didn't feel intentional. It felt more as if something turned my head for me.

I spotted what I assumed must be Sauvie Island in the distance, but I only knew that had to be it because the highway followed the river, and I had just passed a turn onto a bridge. Immediately after that, a short string of houses appeared all in a row and jutting out into a narrow blue channel. On the land above these houses, a parking lot spread out wide and long, bordered by woods.

I'd never even heard of houseboats before and didn't know how to name what I saw, but in the moment that I turned to look, I felt an electric connection. As it turns out, I have only felt that spark a few times in my life. I had no idea then how rare it would be so I simply noted this feeling but didn't take it seriously enough to stop the car.

How was I to know at that young age that such moments wouldn't happen very often? So far, life had been an interesting and sometimes extraordinary experience. One moment you're down the road from your parents' home in the Midwest, sitting in a university writing workshop led by, of all people, the very writer you've admired most in your life; the next, you're sitting in the living room of a Kuwaiti art dealer and sipping from a tiny cup of strong and sweet black coffee while she tells you how the grass in her yard had been flown to the country in strips of turf, unrolled, and then placed neatly upon the sand and watered incessantly; and then you find yourself across the world living with a bunch of activists and opening the first day care center for preschool children in the city, allowing young mothers, many of them single, to earn enough money to pay their rent. And then, on your day off, while driving your young dog to the Oregon coast, along comes some mysterious force that turns your head and whispers, *Look!* Who can tell what can happen, what to expect, what's of lasting significance? At least part of the pleasure of youth is the abundance of surprise and the way your response to it shifts as you grow up, from mute awe to the ability to articulate astonishment, however humbly (I probably muttered "far out" when I spied the houses on water).

And so, because life was always surprising me, I didn't stop to see the houses floating along the mainland and facing the island. I was on my way to the ocean with my new dog, happy that we would soon be running together on the beach. I drove on.

Several years later, tired of living in cramped apartments, I'd started searching for a way out of the city. One morning an ad for a houseboat showed up in *The Oregonian*. I immediately ripped it out. I knew by then what houseboats were, and I wanted somewhere to settle, even if the structure I settled in sat on water. The city, with all its needs and diversions, had swallowed up my life; it was time for a change.

The houseboat for sale was on the same moorage I'd passed on that long-ago drive down Highway 30 when Carson, still at my side, had been a puppy. I walked along a rickety dock amazed by this close-up view of mostly older structures chained to a common wooden walkway. Many boards on the walkway showed signs of rotting, and quite a few were missing altogether, revealing the river moving quickly below. Still, the old dock managed to host a row of power poles, although only a couple of them stood straight. Thick curls of black wire spiraled downward from the stanchions' tops and extended over the walkway to the houseboats. Some of these wires drooped so low over the walkway I felt that maybe I should

duck when I passed under them in order not to be electrocuted.

Under the houseboats and in front of them ran a vibrant blue-green channel of water a quarter of a mile wide. The only human visible was a middle-aged man rowing a small boat, a white cat seated across from him.

Every other direction I turned looked forlorn, almost haunted. I hoped the house for sale was in better shape than many of those I passed. On the way into the property, the realtor had pointed out the remnants of an old mill. A wrecking yard had taken over the few derelict structures that remained. It seemed likely that, way back in the days when the mill had operated, some of the workers may have built at least a few of the houseboats I now saw. It would have been a task to carry freshly milled wood down to the river and set to work, but not an impossible one. Workers could have lived cheaply in houseboats, paying rent to no one and fishing for dinner from their front decks.

Some of the doors on the oldest houseboats hung crookedly. Too many wakes from barges and big boats, along with endless nudging from flowing water, must have rocked the timbers and logs below each of these houses into wonkiness. Cobwebs coated windows. Narrow stovepipes rose like rusted periscopes and leaned precariously this way and that over rooftops. One small house had an arched roof that looked as if someone had sawed a large wooden barrel in half and placed it overhead. (Later I learned this roof was indeed a barrel, specifically a pickle barrel, and this place was known by the neighbors as The Pickle Barrel House.)

Worrisome thoughts about wayward stovepipes, a treacherous walkway with dozens of missing slats, and tipping stanchions with drooping wires nibbled at the corner of my mind. Shouldn't I back away from this houseboat idea? And yet, I thought, how can a place where men take cats for rides in boats be a bad place to live? Besides, there was also that turning of my head years before, that inner voice whispering, *Look!*

And so I continued to step over the gaping holes and walked on, following the realtor. The houseboat for sale—a converted boatwell with a flat, leaking roof, a dodgy electrical system, a wealth of drafts, uninsulated walls, old lead water pipes, and one door so out of whack that a family of otters could have scuttled in under it—turned out to be in worse condition than any of the others. But then again, it came cheap. I still worked in day care and had no

savings, but the mother of the person I was then partnered with had promised us a few thousand dollars toward a down payment. We moved in and set to work replumbing, rewiring, insulating, and making repairs we listed on a stack of index cards that seemed to grow by the hour rather than diminish at the end of each day.

The partner, originally enthusiastic, stayed for less than a decade, but here I remain on the same moorage, though not in the same houseboat, forty years after first stepping onto the walkway. The moorage has changed, I've changed, and the river itself has changed as rivers do—moment by moment—but the constancy of the river's companionship has been the great privilege of my life.

Moorage Backwater, Upriver Houseboats (1990s).

PART TWO

An Anecdotally Illustrated Glossary of Terms

A houseboat is a house that sits on a log and timber float. Strategically placed barrels underneath keep the float up above the water. Living on a houseboat is both the same as living on land and radically different. It's the same because these structures, which are sometimes referred to as "floating homes," at least by realtors, usually stay in one place. You can move your houseboat, but it doesn't happen often.

Most houseboats look like houses you'd see in any city or suburb but, unlike land neighborhoods where one sort of house with minor variations may fill block after block, there's a wide variety in style and condition of houseboats, from rustic to ramshackle to modern. At least this is the case at the moorage where I live and several others in the Portland area.

Here, all twenty-nine houseboats are moored to a common boardwalk, sometimes called "the dock" or "the walkway." Except for some shifting when wakes come along thanks to a barge or speedboat, the houses stay relatively still. That's not to say they don't move at all. First-time visitors almost always notice some unsteadiness. But they don't move around in the same way that a boat, for example, moves in the water. The most immediately noticeable difference between a land neighborhood and a moorage is that water replaces yards and driveways. That, and how people talk.

Maybe the best way to describe what it's like to live on a houseboat is to break that down—how we talk. We use terms that land dwellers may not immediately recognize, and this terminology is important to us. Not only is it important and necessary, but at any time any one of these terms can trigger a memory or story.

Of course these accumulate after decades of living here. So I've decided that the best method to convey what it's like to live on a moorage—at least what it's been like for me—is to let some of our language trigger a few of the stories embedded within it. Even if you don't want to know about something that once happened on a houseboat moorage not far from Portland, at least you'll know how to speak to the people who live on a moorage if you ever happen to go to one.

Heron bathing. Reassembly required.

Backwater: *The runlet between the houseboat walkway and the riverbank.*

The majority of windows on almost any houseboat face the river, but if you're coming by land, you must enter the house from the walkway on the backwater side. The "front door" either faces the walkway or opens on one side of the houseboat.

The backwater itself isn't a separate body of water. It's a stream divided away from the river by the existence of the houseboat moorage. The string of houseboats, held in place by a common walkway, acts as an island. Over the years, our moorage has expanded to include twenty-nine houseboats, allowing for a quarter-mile-long, shallow backwater that's home to plentiful animal life. Muskrats and beavers cruise here. Otter pups tumble on the riverbank with their parents, all of them skittish about humans, except when they're not. If they don't dive immediately out of sight, they'll sometimes swim with curiosity straight toward the houseboat people, who like to stand on the walkway watching them. Weasels and mink are rare; if spotted, they usually scurry under brush to hide from human eyes.

Bald eagles and osprey tend to build nests away from the backwater with its human comings and goings, but they do fly over there to use the uppermost branches of the bank's cottonwoods as perches from which to look for leaping fish below and also beyond the houseboats, out on the river. Blue herons come flapping along to land in these trees, too, but more often they wade in the shallows to find fish, or they perch on logs washed up in the backwater.

Bird life along the backwater and in the skies above is abundant because of the nearby forest and because Sauvie Island, across the channel, is a bird refuge with a huge feathered population: American coots, sandhill cranes, snow geese, trumpeter swans, a variety of owls and ducks, along with raptors including the osprey mentioned above, golden eagles and bald eagles, falcons, vultures, and a wide range of hawks, as well as thousands of smaller birds, from bluebirds and blackbirds to flickers and finches to wrens and warblers—a paradise of birds. The spillover of this winged population from island and forest, over and around the moorage, is an added gift to living here.

A few years ago, a neighbor said he heard the growl of a cougar or possibly a bobcat on the riverbank one spring night. The cat was probably coming down the bank for a drink

Backwater.

and felt alarmed when he spotted a human stepping out onto his backwater-side deck for a smoke. Big cats don't normally come so close, but right across the highway, the forest provides home to several, thanks to a healthy food supply, including deer and elk along with smaller fare: foxes, rabbits, coyotes, rodents, and raccoons.

With its human population and parking lot full of cars, trucks, and a row of stored boats, the moorage is an unlikely place for big cat visits, but now and then coyotes tread along the bank above the backwater, under cover of brush and shady cottonwoods, hoping a domestic cat will emerge from one of the houseboats and slip into the woods. They've been successful in some of these hunts, and when it happens, we grieve. Like Smitty, who took his cat on regular boat rides, many in the human population here love cats. A moorage favorite, Stanley, was a muscular gray tabby who liked to swim from his houseboat across the backwater so he could wander the woods. He never met up with any of the coyotes, or he outsmarted them if he did, and he died of natural causes.

The Canada geese, coots, grebes, and both mallard and merganser ducks easily find meals of seeds and other plant life floating in the backwater and growing on the bank. Beavers like the backwater too. It's a quiet place for them to chew down cottonwoods so they can use the branches to build lodges. They build either downriver close to the bank or under the houseboats, which brings us to the first story of my time here and one of the most memorable.

Ducks in the backwater.

Beavers in the Basement: *A rodential nuisance of houseboat life.*

One of the loudest forms of animal intercourse that can occur underneath a house, even louder than otters mating, is beaver sex. I know this because I've had both—although thankfully not at the same time—mating in my basement, a usually silent, forty-foot-deep, and very wet place. The substructure of a houseboat, a crisscross of logs and timbers called stringers, comprises a raft the house sits on. This raft, or "float" as houseboat people call it, provides a hidden, safe place for birthing.

For some reason, the otters did not like mating under my house and only did it once, but for a spell of several years, the beavers always came back. I'd be awakened in the middle of a winter night by the sounds of enthusiastic grunting,

Beaver lodge.

splashing, and moaning beneath my bedroom, followed in a little while by loud, toothy chomps on the stringers. Because sleep was then out of the question, I would often lie awake wondering about this chomping. Was it the beaver version of a postcoital cigarette? Some form of dental hygiene? Tooth sharpening? It might have been boredom—too late to go gnaw down a tree, too early to forage for leaves, but look here: there's all this timber we could chew.

It had to be one of these, because nothing from heavily masticated timber could possibly be used for lodge building. If you've never heard the sound of beaver teeth sawing on wood under your bed at two or three a.m., you can't imagine its grip on the human brain, especially because the brain can add and subtract. Because of constant exposure to the elements, every so often stringers need to be replaced, either with fresh timbers or with the new, more expensive but longer-lasting steel version. No matter what they're made of, stringers cost thousands of dollars each. This means not only can you lie awake annoyed by beaver sex and aggravated by after-sex grinding of teeth against wood, but you can also work yourself into a worried mess when you consider what these animals are doing to the substructure of your house that will require expensive replacement sooner rather than later.

This beaver activity was the reason I purchased an ultrasound device to repel rodents—which, in case you've forgotten, beavers are. Rodents, according to the booklet that came with the device, can hear the high-pitched sound, but humans can't hear it. The rodents supposedly hate it and flee.

When mating season came around, I tied the device to a cord, draped it over the edge of the deck so that it faced the lodge, and turned it on. The beavers ignored it, and the sexual romping began.

Seeing my desperation to get rid of these animals before they got too far along in the lodge-building and procreation process, a neighbor suggested I hang a light next to the ultrasound device, between the deck and the river, and aim it underneath the house. Beavers hate bright light, she said, and they'll go build their lodge and birth their kits elsewhere rather than try to live with it.

But my beaver couple treated the lamp like a porch light. They used its glow as their preferred entry point and let it guide them deep into the underside of the house and to their twiggy-branchy sex den where they could freely copulate and then indulge in stringer mastication all night long.

The following year I took extreme action. I observed the beavers closely, listened to their noises, and determined they were constructing the new lodge under the bedroom closet, a narrow space with an unfinished plywood floor. I knew my deterrents needed to be closer to where the action was. I decided to saw a hole into the floor.

There's a couple of feet of space between the floor of a houseboat and the river itself, so my plan was to shoo the beavers away with both the ultrasound device and the bright light hanging down under the closet's floorboards, as near as possible to their lodge. After sawing the hole, I walked out onto the deck to retrieve the lamp, and when I came back into the closet and knelt down to begin my work, a beaver popped his head up through the hole and flashed his carrot-colored teeth only inches from my face, so close I could have examined his gums for stringer slivers. Neither of us could have been more surprised. The beaver lowered his head and consulted with his mate about the experience. Some grunting; no moaning.

I slammed the square piece of plywood I'd cut out back into place. Later that day I felt brave enough to return to the scene. I dangled the light and the ultrasonic device down through the opening and clipped them to a bolt so they wouldn't slip and touch the water. I turned both of them on and placed the board back over the hole.

A week or so passed before I admitted defeat. It turned out that these beavers could accept all that light and the beyond-human-range squealing from the ultrasound device nearby. Not even the sight of me with my eyes bugging out of my head had moved them a bit.

But then one day, by chance, something came along that the beavers couldn't tolerate the thought of living near. My friends Teresa and Ruby arrived from Utah for a visit. As soon as she came into the houseboat, Ruby, a black lab, sniffed eagerly at the closet. It was empty. I'd removed all my clothes due to the smell. I explained to Teresa, a human being, that beaver odor is pungent, like nothing you've ever smelled before, even if you're a dog who has smelled a world of disgusting things.

I opened the door for Ruby to show her the hole, and when I lifted the hatch, one of the beavers immediately swam over and rose up over half its impressive length into the narrow space. Ruby looked at the beaver, and the beaver looked at Ruby, and then Ruby raced into the living room and promptly shat on the rug. I scolded the beaver, who dropped quickly back down. He and his partner must have been more perturbed by events this time because shortly after meeting Ruby face to face, they left for good. A slight, pointy-nosed, pinto-colored whippet, a human, and a couple of cats trotting around on the floor above them had been fine for years, but a large black lab's face so close up must have looked like a bear.

The beavers' departure came as a great relief. Shortly before they left, I'd heard that a neighbor down at the other end of the walkway, a secretary at the Marine Corps office named Jo, had become so enraged over losing sleep due to beaver sex under her house that she borrowed a pistol from one of the Marines at work and took to shooting through the floorboards, hoping to kill them. I did not want to become that angry.

Luckily for the beavers, Jo's aim was poor. When she moved out and her houseboat was razed to build a new one, several old beaver lodges between the stringers and logs were exposed. The big rodents, smart as any other rodents, had dodged their deaths by moving a few feet in one direction or another and burrowing in when the bullets came flying.

Now, many years later, if I hear the sound of a broad tail striking the water as I come down the ramp after visiting the city for some evening event, it doesn't mean I'm going to hear rocking and rolling under my houseboat while trying to sleep. It only means that a beaver saw me before I saw him. It means a few wavy circles shimmering in the water under the dock lights are the only glimpse of him I'll catch. It means he's under the surface in the dark swimming toward his lodge downriver somewhere, and it means I'm home.

Canada geese at twilight.

Boatwell: *A garage for boats. Usually a structure with three walls and a couple of feet of decking on all three sides of the interior; a boatwell has a patch of river instead of a floor.*

Some neighbors and I sat peacefully sipping cold drinks one sweltering afternoon in a high-ceilinged boatwell on the moorage. The ceiling was extra high because this particular boatwell usually housed a small seaplane, not a boat, and that day the plane was elsewhere.

While slouched on a deck chair in the shade of a cool boatwell chatting aimlessly with neighbors and nursing a gin and tonic, a person can feel deeply at rest, and so the sight of something large and dark in the shadows that is other than human or fish slowly emerging from the placid water directly at your feet can cause a jolt. We'd all seen many things in the water—never this.

When the thing straightened and rose up higher to reveal the definite shape of a large, sleek head, torso, and arms all wrapped in black, I thought of one of my favorite movies from childhood, *Creature from the Black Lagoon*. But then the head swiveled around to face us, and we could see goggles over human eyes. The diver pulled off his mask to explain he'd been doing some work under a houseboat a few doors down and thought he was going to surface in a different spot altogether. We invited him to join us, and so he did, his flippers leaving monstrous footprints as he made his way to a spare lounge chair and held out one black-gloved hand for a drink.

Michael uses his boatwell as a woodworking shop. Stu works on boats and other projects in his. Once during a heavy snowfall my first winter here, I was surprised to walk past an ancient boatwell and hear a groan. Weighted with more than a foot of snow, the little building tilted suddenly and then rapidly sank before my eyes. In the spring its owners helped it rise again, if not good as new at least still useful.

People do tend to treat these structures like garages. They hang tools on the walls, store freezers out there, and keep propane tanks, firewood, and various gear out of sight of the main house. You can find plenty of boatwells with a kitchen and bathroom at one end, a bedroom that's either in the back or built up on top. Some residents of older boatwells got tired of their tiny living spaces and closed in the fourth wall, creating a living area. My first house, as I mentioned earlier, was a converted boatwell, its full story still to come.

Breakwater: *Any obstruction, natural or otherwise, between the houseboats and the open river. Breakwaters help slow down destructive wakes.*

Wakes cause damage by jostling the logs and timbers that comprise the float a houseboat sits on. Big wakes from speedboats, jet skis, and barges can tilt the pictures on your walls and roll the eggs for your breakfast right off the countertop. If a wake is strong enough, visitors grab for the nearest piece of furniture to steady themselves and start to ask questions about how often houseboat people get seasick; to which the answer, for the majority, is never. Wakes normally don't last longer than a couple of minutes, and at all other times the houseboat moves such an insignificant amount we don't notice.

Many years ago, after the tenants had sued the landlord for various forms of negligence and endangerment several times, and after he eventually lost for good and all and left, a dozen tenants got together and purchased the moorage themselves.

One bright day some of these people got into boats and some stood on the decrepit walkway, and together, with pike poles and ropes, they moved the entire thing, rotten planks and all, from the backwater side out to the riverside and secured it to a row of pairs of ninety-foot-tall wooden poles, or pilings, driven deep into

One of my neighbors, Joan, kayaking alongside the breakwater.

the riverbed and secured with metal bands at the top. When tied together like this, pilings are called "dolphins."

The landlord had paid to have the pilings driven and to create the dolphins. In order to make more money, he'd wanted to build a marina in front of the houseboats, which could have endangered our lives because it would have been impossible to move a houseboat away from the dock—and away from other houseboats—in case of a fire. Obviously a lawsuit was called for that time too.

By securing the old wooden walkway to the long straight row of dolphins, the new owners created a breakwater, leaving wide openings for canoes, kayaks, and boats, including fireboats.

After this change, we began to see new things from our riverside windows, such as otters pacing back and forth along the old walkway and scanning the river's surface for fish. In the winter, mergansers added more color with their red heads and striking black and white feathers. Unfortunately the mallard ducks that once populated the breakwater, too, have now moved on after losing so many ducklings to otters here. Canada geese continue to nest in the breakwater's greenery—an abundance of jewelweed that has claimed it—but otters

hunt goslings too. They sneak up underneath and yank the little gold fluffs underwater.

If you live as close to nature day by day as we do here, you cannot be oblivious to the ways birds and animals feed themselves. You may be leaving for work one morning—as I did, for example, many years ago—and stop when you see several of your neighbors standing helpless and transfixed on the walkway as they watch an eagle on top of a breakwater dolphin tear apart and gulp down a herring gull, the majestic white throat of the King of Birds smeared with blood, which is the way of kings.

One day we all stood in this same silent scream of a mind state when, over and over again, a scrappy mink tried to pull a large white goose, a regular breakwater sitter, down under the river, hoping to drown and eat her or carry her home to kits; meanwhile, the goose scrambled, shrieked, and flapped her wings repeatedly as she fought to rise and return to her rightful place on the breakwater. A few people on the moorage got into kayaks and tried to poke at the mink with their oars while shouting to scare it off. But the intrepid mink persisted. Mink, like otters, belong to the *Mustelidae* family, which has survived on this earth for forty million years.

After a long struggle with this tireless mustelid, the goose, gashed and bleeding, could not keep up her fight. The waving oars and human cries coming at her attacker only pushed the small animal back for a few moments at a time and thus slowed down the inevitable process, making the goose's misery last even longer. When they realized this, the kayakers pulled away, but they stayed nearby. Some of them, along with those of us watching, cried at what we witnessed. It seemed only right to stand by and stay with the goose in her death struggle, to send whatever light we could manage in her direction, all the way to the end.

The white goose had long been partnered with a handsome gray goose. After her death, a resident little girl, Lora, gave this large and lonely gray goose the name Big-Big. Big-Big's head and wings were a soft gray, his chest mostly white, and his feet, beak, and even his eyes, except for inky black irises, the color of persimmons. He also liked the breakwater, but without his mate, he became more human friendly. Soon he was a favorite of Jan, an artist who lived a few doors down from me and fed all the geese and a stream of stray cats. For some reason, people think their unwanted cats and kittens will thrive if dumped near a river. But why? Rats? In forty years I have spied only one actual rat on the moorage,

and his head was as large as any house cat's head. Cats cannot fish and they cannot exist here for long without human intervention. Jan kindly provided that for many years, along with spaying and neutering.

Big-Big and the white goose had been living on the moorage before I came, and after the white goose's death, he stayed on for the next thirty-five years. In spite of the fact that geese mate for life and his mate was tragically gone, this particular goose did find love again.

A pair of Canada geese began to allow Big-Big to travel up and down the channel with them and eventually to join them in other, more intimate activities. This ménage a trois appeared content in the months spent together each year. Big-Big, perhaps overfed, grew plump. Too large to fly and not a member of any flock even if he could have flown, he watched the Canada geese, including his pair of friends, fly off every fall.

The flock's departure left him alone to paddle up and down the channel in front of the houseboats and in the autumnal shadows and reflections of the backwater, on through winter's deluge of rain and occasional snowfalls. The loss of his white goose mate and exit of his new geese partners made him appear, at least to human eyes, sorrowful throughout the winter months. Jan continued to feed him, and some of us did call to him, speak to him, and give him lots of attention and affection, but mere humans cannot address so many important things of this world.

Luckily spring always brought the Canada geese back, and then—happiness! For a couple of years in a row, the female in the ménage a trois laid eggs that hatched into goslings with splotches of gray and white. One of these now remains here year round, just as his father did, and is called Little Big. We who have lived here long enough to know the story of Big-Big say hello when we see him, and we remember his father, who one day disappeared.

I like to think that it happened on a sunny afternoon, when we weren't looking. Big-Big paddled downriver along the center of the channel, past the breakwater, past the last houseboat on the moorage, and past the row of broken-off pilings where boats once tied up to deliver logs to the old mill. On and on he went, until forest rose to his left on the mainland and to his right on the island, and when he reached narrow waters that were all green reflection except for a strip of clouds and blue sky above and before him, his intense black-and-orange eyes gently closed, his feet stopped paddling and came to a halt, and Big-Big slowly rolled to one side, his gray head meeting its final rest on the tide.

Big-Big.

Chase Covers: *Protective covers on the walkway to keep rain, people, and animals away from the water piping system.* (See photo at beginning of Part Two.)

You can't drink the river, so you need a clean water supply, and it must run from one end of the string of houseboats all the way to the other. Some moorages put piping alongside their walkways, parallel to pipes for the sewage system, but at our moorage both sets of pipes run side by side down the middle of the walkway. The water carried to our houseboats is fresh. The sewage taken away goes into a trusted filtering system the innards of which I've never seen nor want to, but I know it's checked regularly by DEQ.

Laying chase covers down the middle of a walkway is not a good plan. The walkway that replaced the old, rotting one is a quarter-mile-long chain of linked concrete slabs secured to a series of sixty-foot-high pilings by pile rings. Brackets, stiff arms, and other hardware all help to hold the walkway in place. The chase covers, however, are free of hardware. These ten-foot-long, narrow, painted planks can't be screwed into place because concrete gives nothing to screw them to, and also, at any time, someone may need to get to the water supply or sewer line quickly to shut things off in order to make repairs. Emergency repairs are seldom necessary, but things happen. The

forceful flow of the river moves everything up and down, giant wakes can break things, and high water can play havoc with weaknesses in pipes.

These chase covers sometimes bow or wriggle out of place, which makes them a tripping hazard. When you step on one, it makes a big noise, because it's basically just a loose plank. When someone too tired or tipsy to care much about anything comes home late at night, you can hear the chase covers banging under their feet like a series of slamming doors. This wakes up sleeping dogs, cats, and humans, and any beavers who haven't gone to bed yet will slap their tails a few times on the water in alarm—*kersplash*! Herons are anxious birds, and they, too, will rise from their logs or the branches of backwater trees, squawking as if the Heron Slayer they've always heard about but have never actually seen has come at last for them. The geese, whose ancestors served as guards within the walls of castles because of the way they vocalize profusely at the slightest hint of intrusion, will take to rustling and flapping and clucking and loudly criticizing the whole situation from their snoozing positions on the breakwater. If, at

29

Blue heron reflection, early evening.

the same time, you throw in the airplane-sized engine of the nightly tugboat pushing a gravel barge as big as a football field upriver, which all of the above can usually sleep right through because everybody's used to it, and you add to all this the howls of annoyed coyotes up in the woods who don't expect slamming doors anywhere near hunting grounds, then that is the end of sweet dreamy dreams for the night.

But most nights, except for the occasional hoot of an owl or two, the forest behind us goes quiet as soon as it's dark. The river wraps up the day's business when darkness settles in too. Traffic along the highway lightens, and no one steps on the chase covers after ten or ten-thirty. Silence falls until dawn.

Dolphin: *Two or more pilings (ninety-foot wooden poles) that have been driven into the riverbed by a pile driver and secured together at the top to form a sturdy triangle (as mentioned in Breakwater above).*

In late fall and early winter, herring gulls arrive to stand on sturdy legs on the tops of the dolphins of the breakwater. From there they can easily scan the river's surface for food. A herring gull's competition for dolphin privileges is the cormorant. Cormorants spend the winter here. A charcoal-colored bird, tall, slim, and funereal, the cormorant flies aggressively toward the dolphin sitter, whether it's a gull or another cormorant, determined to scare it away by speed and some last-minute wingcraft involving quick, belligerent flapping. If the sitter won't budge, the cormorant continues on its way, but if the sitting bird takes flight, the usurper extends both feet to land gracefully on its new perch and spreads arched, pterodactyl-like wings to dry.

Cormorant on a dolphin.

What we view of the dolphins varies. During heavy winter rains and high water, we may see only twenty feet, and the other seventy feet are hidden by the swelling river. In the floods of 1996 and 1997, the river rose nearly to the tops of the dolphins as well as to the tops of the pilings to which the walkway is secured. If more rain had fallen, the walkway—with houseboats attached—would have slipped over the top of all of these poles and floated away from the bank into the channel, down the river, toward the Pacific.

Those of us who lived here during those dangerous times in the 1990s always watch dolphins and pilings carefully now during winter rains. We keep our eyes on the flood markers painted on one of the pilings. If the water rises dramatically but fails to meet the markers, we don't worry.

Dolphin holding up a cloud.

The dolphin-sitting cormorants and gulls don't worry much about anything except food. All they need is a comfortable place to sit and a keen eye to spot fish. It's probably a lot harder to hunt from the water's surface, where you bob along and can only see what's right in front of you and immediately to either side; harder, too, when you have to flap your wings a lot on your hungry flight just above the river.

In spring, a few cormorants linger for a while but most are gone by the end of May. Jewelweed overtakes the logs and planks from the old walkway tied between the dolphins. By summer, this prolific plant will rise up to three or four feet, creating a dense, waterborne hedge of stems, leaves, and bright-yellow flowers on the breakwater. If you go to the parking lot on land above the houseboats, "up top" as we call it, and you enter the woods and run into poison ivy, the jewelweed is a medicine cabinet large enough to make several baths to cure you. It also grows from the logs comprising the rafts beneath the houseboats, but people get in their kayaks and paddle around to clip it off when they see it there because its roots can split the logs, allowing water to seep into the log's interior and speed up decay.

The floating jewelweed hedge at the feet of the dolphins on the breakwater is a hiding place for waterfowl to lay their eggs, for blue herons to freeze in fishing stance and blend in to river and sky while waiting for dinner to swim by, and for red-winged blackbirds to come nest and sing from spring to early fall. One of my neighbors, John, hung several gourd nests for purple martins from a few of the dolphins. The birds love these waterproof, streamlined enclosures and have used them for generations. When I rise early on a summer day and step outside to my upper deck so I can watch the blackbirds and geese take their morning baths and drink from the river as martins and swallows skate across the blue sky, my heart fills with gratitude for my river home.

Blackbird in the jewelweed.

33

Heartbreak: *Yes, it happens, even in this paradise.*

It happens with the loss of animal and bird life we've become attached to, and it happens when we lose people who have walked this dock and looked out upon the river with a range of feelings—curiosity, challenge, interest, wonder, and love. All have made contributions to the rest of us: Smitty, Winnie, Richard, Penny, AJ, Dick, Jo, Lee, Sean, George, Kevin, Jan, and Sharon.

Beloved dogs who kept me company and made days more joyous have died: Carson at fifteen; later Boon, who lived to fourteen; followed by Brio, who was a street dog rescue

The face of the river on a winter day.

34

with congenital kidney disease and died at three. Gone too are the sweetest of cats: Max, Magic, Hadley Mae, and Jazz; all, with the exception of Jazz, lived into their teens. He disappeared, possibly a victim of coyotes.

My parents died, my father at eighty-two in Iowa, and my mother, who lived to be one hundred, here close to me in Oregon. My sister, Marla, died at twenty-seven the year I moved to the moorage; and my brother, Michael, who was my last remaining sibling of three (our oldest brother died by suicide at nineteen), died of cancer at sixty-three. Dear friends have died, and more will die sooner rather than later because we're getting older now. Cousins with whom I imagined always staying in touch have died far away in other states.

And there are loves now gone because it was best. Whenever those skies fell, friends and neighbors helped prop them back up until the day came when I could watch the last of the clouds disappear on my own.

If a river tells you anything, it's that life relies on movement, change, reflection. If you expect it to stay the same one day to the next—one moment to the next—you will suffer. With heartbreak comes gratitude for all the love. Yet there are days, especially in the hard rains of January, the river churning and dark, when gratitude is a dim candle. Sorrow yields to depression. I've watched it happen for me year after year. Partly it's the weather and the threat of snow and ice and the fact of being older now and not managing these things as well as I once did. Partly it's because several of the losses mentioned above happened during Januarys past. No metaphysical messages from nature help me at all through those short days and long nights. It's only that I know from my four decades here that the passage of time will make a difference, even if it doesn't heal all wounds. The river will turn from murkiness and flow silver again in the mornings, green in the afternoons, indigo at twilight. Clusters of wild iris will spring up alongside goslings and red-winged blackbirds on the breakwater. Otter kits will slide down the riverbank again while young eagles, sprung from their aeries, glide over the backwater above them. The island across from the houseboats will turn gold and green; with luck, a couple of deer and a fawn or two will stray down closer to the water to munch on the blackberry bushes there and we can watch them through binoculars. Eventually, when the rain-swollen river lowers, sailboats will wing by; out come kayaks, paddleboards, and canoes. After all these years in its company, when the river shrugs off the weight of winter and relaxes into spring, then summer, so do I.

January afternoon.

Honey Pot: *WWII military slang for toilet, but in this case the term applies to a partially submerged metal or fiberglass container under or next to the houseboat to collect waste. A small motor pumps the waste into the sewage pipe under the walkway.*

If you ever stay at someone's houseboat, or even visit, be extremely careful about what you put down the kitchen sink or toilets. If you're not, the owner may need to dismantle the honey pot in order to get out whatever that thing was that you put in the wrong place, and this is a task you do not want to wish on anyone generous enough to let you enjoy river views and breezes. Sometimes the motor may need to be replaced. This is not cheap.

Actual honey pot.

Most owners post something in the bathroom about this very problem to forewarn guests. If signage is not there, please remember the words on this page.

Layer-cake Boat: *A two- or three-story boat, often with an American flag attached so as not to be mistaken for a ship from a hostile country.*

The larger versions of a layer-cake boat may be a source of hostility—including mine, along with some other houseboat dwellers. This is why: If you're walking along the walkway aware of the fragrance of wet grasses along the bank, a pleasant perfume wafting down from the lilac bush at the top of the ramp, the dizzying scent of daphne rising to greet you as you pass by Deborah and Michael's place, and suddenly you catch a whiff of gasoline that overpowers all of the above, it's probably coming from a great big layer-cake boat. The term was coined at this moorage by resident and dear friend, Jim, a guy with a knack for getting things right.

A layer-cake boat is often named something cute like Ezy-Duz-It or Dreems-Come-Tru and manned (literally) by one person, although man and wife, man and mistress, or man and someone he's hoping to seduce are often spotted sitting together in the vicinity of a wheel. The purpose of a layer-cake boat is to impress and to use up some natural resources for the sake of one or two people having a fun day steering an enormous, gas-guzzling object down a river and creating wakes for kayakers to maneuver through.

Because I'd like this term to catch on, I'm including it in this glossary.

Jim.

List: *To lean to one side; a term usually applied to boats, but it happens with houseboats too.*

Not only did its flat roof leak, my first houseboat tilted dramatically on the downriver side because the previous tenants, a couple of fishermen, had installed a massive brick fireplace without first putting in adequate flotation (underwater support in the form of air-filled barrels). In those early days, if Carson stood in the upriver corner and missed when I tossed her a ball, the ball would roll speedily downward toward the fireplace and into its charcoal-littered mouth, from which cold air streamed steadily due to the mysterious lack of a damper.

Combined with the uninsulated walls, the chill in the living room made that first winter feel like camping in the rain on Mt. Hood. Buckets placed strategically caught drips, but not all of the flooring was safe enough to hold buckets of water. Because the house had originally been built as a boatwell, the float—that crisscross of logs and stringers—did not provide support for a large portion of the living room, and much of the old wood floor had gone soft with rot.

That spring, the first priorities were to replace the flooring and dismantle the fireplace, which revealed marijuana seeds behind several of the bricks. Maybe the former tenants had built this useless monstrosity in order to create a hiding place for their pot seeds. Dried now, some of them burnt, they couldn't produce much of a crop.

New plywood replaced the floor; sheetrock replaced the bricks. A diver installed new flotation, and the listing houseboat, which was never in danger of sinking, was righted.

More than thirty years later, after I'd moved into a new houseboat and an unusually heavy snow fell one winter, sinking did become a threat.

After a snowstorm came rain, followed by freezing temperatures. This made a frozen cake of snow on my slanted roof. More snow, more rain, more freezing nights came along quickly on the tail of that first storm, and an even weightier cake pressed down on the rooftop. The houseboat began to list in an unnerving way.

One of my nearby neighbors, Steve, climbed up onto Father Pat's flat roof next door to remove as much snow as he could, then turned to my house. Father Pat, actually a monk not a priest, had lived among us for many years, but he was by then too old to climb up onto his roof safely or else I'm sure he would have done so. He looked on worriedly from the walkway as Steve stepped precariously along the edge of his roof and used a long-handled shovel to try to pull down some of the heavy snow on my roof, which he would let drop into the river. As he did this, I shoveled off my decks to rid the house of weight, but the ice coating made things difficult. Nevertheless, we felt that this would help with the list, and it did somewhat. Unfortunately, the roof is shaped in such a way that Steve couldn't get to anything beyond the edges, and I couldn't get below some of the deeper layers of ice. Most disturbing of all, snow continued to fall.

At around eleven that night, the snowfall had stopped. I was about to breathe a sigh of relief when I heard an ominous creaking sound. I walked outside to look around just as two neighbors, John and Morgan, who lived at opposite ends of the moorage, happened to be passing by together. Both stopped in the icy darkness lit only by a walkway lamp and looked at the state of my house with me.

Thanks to all the new snow, the house now listed so badly on the front, upriver end that one corner nearly touched the water. Should snowfall continue, the structure could topple.

They assessed the situation for only a few seconds before starting to plot a course of action.

I knew my houseboat was in good hands. By using a combination of nautical and engineering skills combined with serious human muscle power along with unmatched can-do attitudes, these two undaunted men have gotten me and others on the moorage out of scrapes too numerous to mention over the past decades. I felt so lucky they happened to be passing, because I was in a state of shock.

John said he'd need to go home and get some ropes, and Morgan went to get another shovel. Before he left, John urged me to go inside and move furniture from the upriver corner to the opposite end of the house, in other words to create ballast. His voice was calm and reassuring, but I knew because of this single direction that the situation was dire.

I called my neighbor Julia down the way, and she hurried over to help me move tables, chairs, and cabinets to the middle of the living room.

Meanwhile, John and Morgan brought ropes, snow shovels, flashlights, and a plan. They worked for the next few deeply cold hours to assure my house would stay in place and not tip any further. By around three in the morning, after much shoveling, scraping, hoisting, wedging, pulling, and tying up, they left me with a house as secure as it could be until more flotation would bring it up out of the water to its normal level. When, thankfully, the sun came out the next day, Jesse, our on-land neighbor, helped push this project in the right direction by moving heavy planters to the far corner of my deck to provide more ballast and climbing up onto my steep roof to shovel away heaps of snow.

Julia, who had helped move the furniture, was a relative newcomer to the moorage. Two years after this event, she remarked that she hadn't really understood what it meant to be part of a houseboat community until that frightening night. Maybe ours is not much different from other moorages in terms of coming together in emergencies, but I do believe there are some special people here, and many of them have performed kindnesses to others in the neighborhood over the years.

Some examples from my own life: My neighbor Tim drove me in his van to pick up a new-to-me but very old (1957) ten-foot skiff at a marina downriver one day. When we realized I couldn't rely on its tired motor to get the boat and me safely back upriver, he simply picked

it up—a boat!—and put it in his van, shut the doors, brought it (and wide-eyed me) back to our moorage, and showed me how best to tie it up. Tim's wife, Sandra, leaves delicious squash soup, cheesecake, peach cobbler, and an array of other treats at my door, each time whisking herself away on (usually) bare and silent feet. When I used to chop my own wood, Steve, a chiropractor (the same Steve who climbed up onto Father Patrick's roof) unfolded a worktable in his living room and fixed my out-of-whack back at least once or twice every winter. Downriver from him, another Steve, a former police officer, is famous for having pulled several dogs out of the river when they accidentally fell in, including my dog, Boon.

Once, after an afternoon windstorm, I looked outside and saw that one of the kayaks usually at rest on my swim float was missing. I put out an email asking neighbors to keep a lookout but had little hope. Not long after hitting send, I glanced outside again and saw Patricia and Tim (another Tim), two intrepid, skilled kayakers, with their paddles flying as they sped downriver. Soon they appeared by my swim float holding a rope tied to my missing kayak as if it were a wayward pony. And then there was the foresight and kindness of another neighbor, Ron. When the electricity went out a few times during one long winter, I began to worry about heavy snow, wind cutting the power, and having no heat because my only source is a heat pump. Ron suggested a backup, a propane stove like the one he and his wife, Carole, use. He gave me the specs, I ordered it, and he drilled the holes, hooked up the pipes and hoses, and made sure I knew how to use it before he left. Father Patrick once pulled my one and only outdoor lounge chair out of the river after another storm and saved it for lounging in another day. Jim and Melissa have invited me in to share a meal when they saw me passing by on a walk. Only yesterday, Joan offered help with a project I'm working on. Morgan has come to my aid at all times, day or night, to help with anything and everything from leaky faucets to removing a water heater that had met its end. The wet pool I'd been unaware of under that water heater had wrecked a good deal of the utility closet's floor, which Jesse chopped out and replaced with plywood and which Michael, a fine woodworker, then covered with smooth, new flooring. Stu once came over and lifted a post that had gone wonky on my deck and jimmied it back into place, all the while laughing at the $1,500 bid that a contractor had given me to do exactly what he was doing.

This is a place of great generosity. Salli listens carefully to what interests people and drops off appropriate articles, recipes, coupons, and more in on-deck (as opposed to postal service) mailboxes. Julia bakes magnificent apple cake, chocolate cake, and cookies and shares all freely, while Stu can solve any boat issue a boat can come up with. Carol knows everything there is to know about plants; her husband John is as knowledgeable about birds. I could go on, but it would be impossible to list all who have reached out to help me and to help each other. If there's ever money exchanged for such kindnesses, it's usually minimal.

There are twenty-nine houseboats here, and they hold artists, animators, social workers, labor organizers, doctors, nurses, filmmakers, tavern owners, construction workers, pilots, mechanics, tech workers, photographers, teachers, truck drivers, and more. Each day they show up to make the moorage the pleasurable place to live that it is, and when anyone's life, body, or houseboat may be listing, they show up for that too.

Morgan's door.

Midstream: *A spot in a river where you're not supposed to change horses, but it's okay to change houseboats there.*

After spending thousands of dollars year after year on house insurance, moorage rent, upkeep, and most draining of all, expensive repairs for a place I didn't even own and in which the legal owner no longer took any interest—money I'd never be reimbursed for—I decided to move. Mostly it was the roof that defeated me. I'd started to curse it even in my dreams. The best I could foresee was more patching or else forking over $17,000, the lowest estimate from contractors who told me they could rip the thing off and start again. That was a sum I didn't have, which meant I'd need to borrow it, and I knew there would never be repayment for that small fortune either. The latest roof rain coat I'd purchased for the old houseboat, a thick, creamy, white substance advertised as waterproof and more or less good for eternity, had cost $3,000 and lasted only two years before the leaks started again.

When my beloved Aunt Mattie died and left me some money from the sale of her small house in North Dakota, the home I'd lived in for some years as a child and that she'd lived in for sixty years, I knew it would have pleased her if I'd use the inheritance to move on. She had long wanted me out of that ever-needy house. I knew that no matter how much more money I poured into it, the old houseboat would continue to outwit me. It was a house of cards. Even if something could be fixed, there was always the next thing waiting for attention including, most expensively, the float, which had been pounded for half a century or more by boat wakes. If a roof cost $17,000, a full set of new stringers could be four or five times that. One day I was trying to fix the shower floor and glanced over to see the toilet sitting slightly lopsided and needing immediate attention before it sank through the rotting floorboards. All sorts of problems involving walls, doors, floors, and ceilings haunted that house. Another day I discovered a cluster of dangerously exposed electrical wires hanging above the front door, installed and then tucked out of sight by an electrician's apprentice who'd lived there and hadn't quite known what she was doing.

I decided the most practical next step would be to move back to land. Land appreciates in value, I reasoned, but the water rights for houseboats are leased and will never belong to the people living on the river. I'd just need to be tough with myself, get practical, and leave the river behind.

A friend recommended a realtor, a calm middle-aged gentleman who showed me house after house in Portland. Each time we entered another front door, I walked straight to the living room window and saw only grass, sidewalks, and cars—cars parked in the streets, cars in driveways, cars speeding by. No geese. No ducks. No backwater with otters rolling down the bank. No raptors overhead. No woods. No boats. No herons. And who were those people on the sidewalks ignoring each other even as they passed? Could you ever really know them? Could their kindness possibly run as deep as that of my river neighbors? Could you count on them? I'd mutter about all this to the realtor at each house. After ten or so houses, he gently pointed out that perhaps I didn't want to leave the river.

By this time, the moorage was equipped for twenty-nine houseboats, not one more. Miraculously, an empty slip opened up because one of the residents had sold her houseboat and the buyer hooked it up to a tug and took it away to Washington. I read this as a fortunate event, a sign that I didn't need to go back to the land after all. I'd buy a better houseboat and move it into the empty slot. My friend and neighbor Salli went with me to look.

One of the first houseboats for sale that we saw had a tiny kitchen and a wooden ladder shooting almost straight up: living room on the second story and another, more slanted and commodious ladder leading to a bedroom on the third. I climbed willingly and enjoyed each view, but I was in my fifties and couldn't imagine growing old in a house that required scrambling up and down ladders.

Ladders, it turned out, were the least of it. New houseboats are costly to build, the city won't make room for them, and existing moorages are mostly full. So that left a lot of old floating homes on the market. Rotting boards comprised the decks of too many to count. Green, orange, or blue shag carpeting covered wooden floors soft as sponge. Paint peeled liberally. Creaking doors opened onto rooms tacked on without thought in spots that made no sense—a kitchen where you'd expect a living room, a utility room up a few steps behind a bathroom.

Salli and I made our way in and out of well over a dozen houseboats advertised in a Portland marina newspaper. To get into one of them, we had to enter by skirting the fifteen-inch-wide outside deck of a boatwell then staggering from one handrail to the next, and there weren't that many of them. A narrow tool room filled with rusty boat parts and half-finished projects acted as the entrance for another. The owner explained to us he'd need to leave all that behind. Shrugging his shoulders, he guessed I'd have to deal with it if I wanted to buy. Another house looked almost like a pyramid and smelled as if patchouli oil had seeped into the walls. Up near Ridgefield, Washington, we came upon a round house with a little lookout room and a widow's walk tacked on top. Interesting, but too big and too costly to tug all the way downriver to the open slip on my moorage. I fell in love with a tiny place painted red, narrow as a railroad car and oozing 1950s décor inside, including a large mahogany box containing a wee TV screen. I liked the black-and-white diamond pattern of the linoleum floor in the kitchen too, but I knew that floor would feel like a block of ice beneath my feet come winter. The cold river just isn't that far away. Also the plumbing, the owner admitted, "needed work." In the house I was living in, I'd learned how to glue PVC joints and solder copper pipes while stuffed partway into a cubby under the kitchen sink, but I didn't ever want to replumb a house again.

People buy houseboats because they're far less expensive than houses on land. You're not getting that valuable and irreplaceable chunk of real earth, a piece of the planet with your name on the deed. Many whose homes Salli and I entered lived right next door to poverty. I tried to smile at one man as I walked under a drooping living room ceiling and caught sight of buckets for rainwater tucked into corners and under beds so that potential buyers wouldn't guess the roof was an issue—in case they failed to see it. I still owned and used buckets like those. I could see the despair and frustration in the owner's eyes: *Buy this place so I can get out of here.*

But a fixer-upper, after so many years of upping and fixing, was not for me.

When the height of summer rolled around, Salli got busy with her kids, her own house, and her art projects; she dropped out of the search. After only a week or two on my own, finding a place felt lonely and hopeless. I decided to call a houseboat realtor.

With Salli, the realtor, the realtor's assistant, and on my own, all together I'd looked at over one hundred houseboats before the assistant, after driving me around for yet another long day of fruitless hunting, decided to take me to a moorage a few miles upriver from home. The search had been going on since early fall, and it was now winter. I could feel her frustration increase with her growing silence on these car rides. I was certain that soon she'd give up on me because I wouldn't settle for something I didn't love, something that I guess her other clients felt delighted to do. But I'd had enough of living in a house that refused to be happily inhabited. I was prepared to do normal maintenance, but I didn't want to repair one more thing, or pay someone else to repair it—not for a long while anyway. "But houseboats can be quirky," she kept reminding me, as if I didn't know. As we drove into the parking lot of yet another moorage, she told me that, given my fussiness—I believe she came right out and used that term—any place on her listings now would be a "long shot" for me.

I looked at the sheet of paper she offered describing the history of the long shot we were about to visit. It had been on the market for a while at a price out of my range, she said. But recently, she pointed out with one sharp red nail poking at the paper, the price had dropped. When I saw the new price, I stifled a groan. Even with the owner's reduction by $15,000, it was still out of reach. By the end of this discussion, we'd already parked, so I thought it worth a look at least.

The moment I saw the little forest-green house with white trim, two bright-red kayaks hanging on one of the outer walls, I knew it was mine. I almost ran down the ramp to greet it. I wanted to throw my arms around it. Of course it was

mine! Another price drop possibly achieved through some bargaining would mean I could afford it. After all, thanks to Aunt Mattie and a new job that actually paid a salary that even allowed for a savings account, maybe I could pull together enough cash for negotiations to succeed.

The little house was exactly what I'd been describing to both the realtor and the assistant for months: small with a loft, new or remodeled. All the forced shuffling across shag carpeting, the steep ladders, the squishy floors, the hopeful smiles while being led into kitchens where living rooms ought to be and living rooms with no heat source and tiny windows—every bit of the journey now felt worth it if I could live in this house.

I shook with excitement as the realtor punched in the code on the lockbox, and I walked in a giddy daze all around the tiny, pristine interior while listening to the story of how two men had bought this old houseboat on the cheap as their weekend getaway. They'd torn it down to the studs; rebuilt it with brand new wiring and plumbing (yahoo!); painted it beautifully inside and out; added three sets of French doors opening out onto decks, upper and lower; put in a skylight and a twenty-foot-wide swim float, or floating deck, out front where they could sit for hours and enjoy the river close up…and then they'd adopted a toddler together. On his first visit, the little boy took off running across the swim float toward the river. One of the men grabbed him just in time. The two frightened dads looked at each other and decided immediately to sell.

Even if this was a big fib to cover for two guys flipping a house, I didn't care. Every door opened smoothly. Every cabinet hung perfectly straight. Instead of only one working burner (on my stove from the 1960s), all four burners in this kitchen glowed bright red when I turned them on. Drawers glided open with the slightest touch, gleaming white inside. Both toilets, one up and one down, sat up straight on hardwood floors. I looked around for the woodstove that would require the hauling and splitting of wood night and day through winter for another twenty-five years and spotted a thermostat on the wall of the living room. *A thermostat for an energy efficient heat exchanger!* And though the sky poured while I swooned from room to room, no rust-orange streaks and splotches covered the ceiling. The brand-new roof—slanted, not flat—kept the rain outside where it belonged.

A few days later, I scrawled my name across the bottom of every piece of new-homeowner paper shoved my way.

A tug brought my new houseboat downriver and maneuvered it successfully into the empty slip, thanks to a lot of helpful shoving with pike poles, heave-ho's, and pulling with ropes by workers and neighbors skilled in such placement. Soon it was chained to the walkway. This took an entire day, but that night I slept under the skylight in my own home. As I started to drift off, I had a moment of panic when I remembered that, long ago, someone had told me skylights were notorious for leaking, but it's been almost two decades of living here now and so far not a drop. All is well, even better than well. I still have the two red kayaks that hung on the side of the house when I first saw it, along with a container garden and outdoor tables and comfortable chairs for both the upper and lower decks.

Walking by my old houseboat on a cold day this past winter, I saw branches from four different beaver lodges sticking out from under one side. I guess the old grandfather and grandmother beavers must have passed on to their great lodges in the sky-river, or whatever beaver heaven may be, without telling their grand-kits about Ruby the bear. I kept right on walking, heading home.

Ramp: *A bridge connecting the walkway to land.*

We have two: one blue, one green. When I first moved here forty years ago, we also had two: one gunmetal gray and the other a couple of old-growth logs jimmied together and tied with heavy ropes. Slats hammered horizontally across the length of the logs made a track for walking, though it felt more like hiking.

A couple of old-timer residents, now gone, told me not long after I first moved in that an angry former tenant blew up whatever structure had served as a ramp before the logs got hauled in. The story was that he'd done it as an act of defiance against the negligence of the greedy landlord. However, it left him and other residents at his downriver end of the moorage with a dangerous replacement. It wasn't easy to climb up and down logs tied together, even with the horizontal boards in place. It remained a long time because the landlord, already slow to repair even the simplest things, wasn't going to rush to rebuild an entire ramp.

So this was the ramp I ascended daily to get to my car and drive to work as a temp at a state office in an historic building downtown. Everyone dressed up for work in those days at the Pittock Building, even temporary, agency-supplied, bureaucrat impersonators like me.

By this time, most of the "steps" on the logs of the ramp had wriggled loose, and so every morning I put on a pair of Timberland boots to climb it and then slipped into my fancy work shoes when I reached the car.

A sturdy metal ramp eventually took its place and was one day painted dark green by Lora, the child who'd named Big-Big years before. By then, Lora was a teenager looking for odd jobs.

Years passed during which we had a green ramp and an old gray metal ramp that wasn't as structurally sound as the green one, but serviceable. Then one day, after a winter's worth of heavy rains had thrummed, soaked, and massaged the earth into a stupor of mud, puddles, and mush, this situation changed.

Carson had died, and my gentle companion was a greyhound/lab mix. That day of the big change, Boon and I had climbed the green ramp in search of some fresh air and good sniffing. His interests lay with grass and then the posts that held up the community mailboxes. My nose led me straight into the arms of the lilac bush nearby. Next, we visited the recycling shed to drop off newspapers and

Downriver ramp in early spring.

cardboard, and on our return Boon wanted to go the long way home, so we walked down the old metal ramp. Seconds after we reached the walkway, a huge cottonwood let loose a booming, cracking cry and crashed down onto the ramp we'd just descended. The top of the ramp took the force of the tree's twitching branches and immediately caved but didn't fall all the way, which left the massive trunk hanging suspended over the backwater. Its traumatized roots waved like octopus arms for a full two minutes and dispersed clumps of coal-black soil the size of soccer balls onto the riverbank and into the backwater.

It turns out it takes a long time to replace a ramp destroyed by a tree because first you have to reduce the size of the tree by cutting it up into large chunks, which are then carted up to the land and cut again into smaller pieces for firewood. After that, time passes as you wait for someone to come and remove the damaged ramp—sixty-some feet of metal—and carry it away. Meanwhile, a new ramp must be assembled in some distant structure by welders, etc., and finally someone needs to install it. In a town and environs with two rivers and twelve bridges, all such people can be found. Eventually.

Months passed with only one access to land,

a reversal of the early days when residents at one end of the moorage could walk up a metal ramp and some of us had to slip, slide, and scramble up two logs laid side by side in order to get to the parking lot or walk the extra distance and choose, as several of my neighbors on the downriver end did, the old metal ramp.

Not too long before the tree fell, some new residents had moved in, and they parked their cars, along with the rest of us, at the end of the graveled parking lot where we could all use the intact green ramp. As we drove to work and came back home and picked up our mail from the community mailboxes, this common ramp gave us a way to know each other better.

Once in place, the new ramp was painted blue, and the whole community had easy access to land and walkway. All the cars spread out again to their appropriate places in the parking lot.

Order returned, and the event was forgotten. Maybe, from time to time, it popped up as a scrap of a story told to a visitor on someone's deck while drinking beer and watching boats go by. But for a quite a long time, the two of us, Boon and I, had a habit of hurrying past the group of trees that stood at the top of the fallen ramp. We'd known the moment we heard that crash behind us the day the cottonwood fell that we'd narrowly escaped our own ends.

In winter, when the rains come and the water rises, the ramp naturally rises too. Instead of its forty-five-degree or steeper angle of summer, it can rise so high it stretches almost level across the backwater, making the trudge to the parking lot much easier. More television stations are available in winter because the houseboats rise and antennae pick up more stations. There is no cable access here, although some people acquired satellite dishes before companies put a stop to their workers climbing around on houseboat rooftops. In summertime, with much less rain and lower water, favorite programs disappear.

Boon became companions with a new neighbor's dog, Molly, a black, gold, and white terrier. Molly helped her friend forget about dangerous trees. Their favorite game was to race up one ramp, cross the parking lot on the path that hugged the riverbank, and hurtle down the other, then fly along the walkway back to the first ramp: up, over, and down again, many times a day.

People carry all sorts of things up and down the ramps: groceries, garbage, recycling, wheelbarrows of wood, pellets, or propane gas tanks for heating stoves, construction materials, giant boxes of fruits and vegetables from the island farms for canning, furniture, refrigerators and other appliances, paintings, mattresses, and all else you can imagine would go into and out of a house anywhere else. New babies have been carried down those sixty feet with care to start their residency here. They've grown and gone up the ramps and off to college or to new lives of all sorts and come back down the ramps with or without partners, a few with babies of their own. Now I watch new toddlers inspecting the walkway accompanied by their grandparents who have lived here almost as long as I have. Tiny fingers point:

"What dis?"

"That's a chase cover."

"What dis?"

"That's a piling."

"What dis?"

"That's the backwater."

Strife: *Disagreement; discord. Wherever people are, there it is.*

Shortly after I came here, my next-door neighbor at the time told me about newlyweds who'd moved into their houseboat, bought everything they needed, settled in, and began blowing up at each other almost every day. One night, angry about money spent on appliances, the husband threw them all into the river: the washer, the dryer, the refrigerator, the toaster, microwave, hairdryer, anything that plugged in. His furious wife walked out onto the deck, looked him in the eye, removed her wedding ring and dropped that into the river too. The next day, after making up, they hired a diver who miraculously found the ring but expressed dismay at what he saw underwater and tried to talk to them about pollution. They shrugged and told him they'd buy new appliances.

This had happened in the early 1970s. I asked if anybody had ever tried to get the appliances out of the river and was told no, but they all felt relief when the couple moved out a few months after the big fight, which had been followed by many smaller but noisy fights.

By the time I moved in, a couple in their sixties— I'll call them Dixie and Martin—had been living on the moorage for ten years. Dixie was friendly, creative, and fond of crafts. She spent her time making doll clothes, afghans, and quilts. Martin, more reclusive, was rumored to have been a brilliant contributor to the early days of the tech industry and was now frustrated by retirement. He drank all day and tried to provoke Dixie into fights. Dixie was smart but not strong. She confided in Lou, a woman who lived at the other end of the walkway. Lou and I were also friends.

Dixie couldn't leave, Lou told me many years after the event I'm about to describe. Those were the days when many women still felt obliged to remain married no matter what. Even though she couldn't allow herself to pack up, Dixie felt certain that emotional and psychological abuse might be all she'd know for the rest of her life.

One night after Martin had been shouting drunkenly off and on at his wife for several hours, he went out in the rain to tie up a boat. A strong wind was causing it to bang noisily against the deck. After a few minutes, Dixie heard him calling her name. When she opened the door and peered out into the dripping night, she saw nothing. Then she spotted a bright globe sinking into the black water at her feet. It took a few seconds to realize she was looking at the top of Martin's bald head.

Dixie paused then knelt slowly down until her knees touched the wooden boards. "His head went down once, and up it came," she later calmly told Lou.

Lou nodded.

"It went down twice," Dixie said. "Up it came." She took a deep breath, exhaling slowly. "Three times. Up it came." She hesitated, thoughtful. "And it was then—that third time—I realized that I'm not a murderer."

After Dixie leaned forward, extended her arms, and helped Martin out of the river, I like to think he never looked at her the same again and that he treated her well, maybe with fear in his heart. But I can only hope this happened because they moved to land and I never saw them again.

A main source of strife for many years was the man who owned the moorage when I arrived. He lived in a trailer at the top of the old metal ramp. Even after many complaints, he failed to replace missing boards on the walkway or raise the hanging electrical wires, and of course he did not replace the ramp made of logs. He wouldn't even replace a broken light bulb on the dock lights attached to pilings that light our way home. This last bit of indifference to his tenants' well-being was especially hard for working residents at the downriver end who came home after dark. We not only had to navigate those two slippery logs and the funky slats for steps, but once we'd accomplished that, we had to tread carefully along a treacherous walkway beneath light poles that may or may not have working bulbs.

At that time, a young man named Karl had lived on the moorage for a long time. Karl liked to hang out in bars for a couple of hours after work, but one night he stayed too long and drank far too much. It took all the concentration he could manage within his beery haze to make it safely to his houseboat on the far downriver end of the moorage. Eight lights should have guided him, but only four of them worked. Once home he found himself sitting on the bed loading his pistol. He stepped outside, stumbled along the treacherous walkway, and shot out three of the last four working bulbs. This "spite your face" activity didn't go over well with his neighbors, including me. I began to wonder about the blown-up ramp story. Could Karl have been the culprit there too?

Karl and the former landlord no longer live here. I heard that both Dixie and Martin died long ago, neither at the hands of the other as far as anyone knows. The newlyweds are probably working on their third marriages by now and their umpteenth set of household appliances. Through the years, some friendships between residents broke and never found their way to mending, but the people who know they don't get along well still tend to make polite conversation in passing anyway because we're all aware that we're part of this small community. Besides, except for some choppy waters now and then, the river serves as a peaceful guide to good living. Equanimity among us reigns—at least for the moment.

Cormorants giving each other space.

Swim Float: *A floating wooden deck attached to the houseboat with chains.*

People who live on houseboats almost always have a problem with space. You have no basement, of course, usually no attic, and perhaps, as is my case, only one or two small closets. To compensate, many people add a swim float as an extra deck on the river level and use it for a variety of purposes: relaxation, including diving into the water on a hot day; container plants; patio furniture; boat storage; tool storage; summer dining; large gatherings, such as groups of friends who want to watch the annual passing of the brightly decorated Christmas boats; and more.

Wilbur and Charlotte enjoying the view from the swim float.

About three decades ago, one of my neighbors, Salli, hankered for a tree on her swim float. She cut a hole in it, planted a young curly willow in a basket of dirt, dropped the basket through the hole, and tied it in place. The tree's roots eventually shot down through the dirt into the water, where a constant supply of nutrients still feeds them, thanks to all the fish and animal life in the river.

A few other neighbors took note of Salli's ingenuity and did the same, and now we have both riverside and backwater swim floats with healthy trees growing up out of them, providing not only shade but branches for finches, robins, red-winged blackbirds, martins, and swallows to hop about. One neighbor planted an alder on his small backwater float, but it grew large and lopsided and finally tipped over, taking the

My neighbor Jiggs on his swim float.

float with it, leaving only a few boards above water. Luckily the backwater at the time was shallow, so the float owner and some helpers pulled everything upright again with the help of a come-along.

A hard wind blowing all night long once caused the current to move so fast that it yanked free one of the chains from the upriver side of my swim float, which is twenty feet by twenty feet. Before I'd gotten out of bed the next morning, I received a call from my next-door neighbor, Tim. "Your swim float has come over for a visit."

When I looked outside, there it was, still partly hooked up to my house but mostly snuggled up against Tim and Sandra's swim float. Luckily the downriver current by then had grown sluggish, so no harm done. Tim got into a boat with some ropes and a visiting relative who could hardly believe his luck at getting to join in on an actual houseboat adventure, and they wrangled the float back into place and hooked it up again with heavier chains.

On my swim float I keep a table and chairs close to the house for easy access when entertaining friends and two deck chairs closer to the side where the breakwater is. These are for viewing bird life and reading. A large orange metal pig I've named Wilbur always stands on the swim float alongside a slightly smaller but still enormous metal spider named Charlotte. Nearby is a tall strawberry bush that my cat, Riley, likes to sit under to watch birds and boats. If it's raining, sometimes she sits under Wilbur.

Riley is a jumbo gray-and-white cat. She spent her first two years in a crowded apartment with a view of one tree next to a small deck, some buildings, and a parking lot. A family had adopted her as a kitten, but after a few years, they got a dog and decided the apartment felt too crowded. I found her on Craigslist and brought her home.

During the five years she's lived here, she's never failed to run to the window to see the gravel barge go by. The long floating tray carrying a mountain of rocks must seem a spectacular sight. The tugboat that pushes the tray along is taller than all the other tugboats she's ever seen on the river and it holds a person, or at least a half person, which is all she can see because he's practically up in the clouds. The tug and the rocky mountain move straight down the center of the narrow channel.

The barge can come day or night, sometimes both day and night. Its timing is hard to predict. To me, the tug's engine sounds like a hydroplane on the river as it pushes its cargo past us, but maybe to Riley it's like the purr of a colossal cat. During the day, she hears this engine coming long before I do, long before the barge is even in view, and she hurries out onto the swim float. From her perspective, this gigantic thing must look as if it comes from out of nowhere, passes the hodgepodge of houseboats on our moorage and the fancier houseboats at the moorage next door, and then goes under the bridge and on into some other nowhere upriver. When this happens during sleeping hours, she's not so interested, unless it comes before she has drifted off. If she's still wide awake, she rushes again to look. At night, with its blinking red and green lights, the whole thing is even more interesting.

Riley's tail.

Once, early on in her residency here, I went out onto the swim float with Riley when the barge came. I explained that moving gravel from place to place is part of human life, but she didn't care what I thought. For all I know, she's made up her own religion by now about the gravel barge with its high priest, its unfathomable origins, purpose, power, and meaning. It lives in her mind in capital letters, and it works in mysterious ways.

Tender House: *A small structure that sits on its own float behind or beside a houseboat, although sometimes a tender house is built upon the same float as the house.*

A tender for a boat is a smaller boat that services it, takes passengers to land, and picks up food and other goods. Long ago, river dwellers gave the same name to the little buildings you sometimes see floating behind, or sometimes alongside, the larger house. Like the mill workers and fishermen who may have built some of the early houseboats on this moorage, marginally employed and poor people all along the waterfront in old Portland found it easy to live on a houseboat and fish for their dinners, and many added tender houses to give them a bit of extra room.

Fishermen kept gear in tenders and used them to store wood and tools. Houseboat people

Joan's tender house.

still use tender houses for these purposes, but they're also used as studios, woodshops, storage for water toys like paddleboards and water skis, as well as the same type of overflow that land dwellers keep in basements and garages.

Approximately one-third of the tender house belonging to one of my neighbors, Joan, is a laundry room. She converted the other two-thirds into a bedroom and once rented it out from time to time with a caveat: no children and no pets. One day a man with two children came by to see if he might rent it. She pointed out that a room the size of a large closet wasn't big enough for the three of them, but he assured her he wanted to rent it for his girlfriend; their children would live elsewhere.

The girlfriend moved in. A few days later, Joan heard barking. When she walked out to the tender house, she saw the woman and her children handing four small white dogs through the tender's window to the boyfriend on the walkway. "The dogs are supposed to be in the van," the woman told Joan. But had the dogs decided on their own to escape the van, run down the ramp, and leap in through the window of Joan's tender house? This was a sad day for those of us who would have liked four small white dogs living nearby. (We're lucky to have one anyway. His name is Jiggs, and I get to live right next door to him.)

Joan's one-story houseboat is built in an early style rarely found on the river anymore, and the tender matches it: the same curved roof for the easy cast of a fishing net to dry, the same low ceiling. Houseboats like this once dotted the waterfront, but most of them, even with the luxury of a tender house, amounted more or less to simple shacks. Only the sturdy and well-built ones like Joan's remain, and they're treasured for their authenticity.

Moving a tender house downriver.

Upriver and Downriver: *Directions used to describe from whence the river comes and to whence it goes.*

The Willamette river begins south of Eugene, Oregon, and wriggles its way north, eventually cutting the city of Portland into two parts: east side and west side. It flows on in a northwesterly direction until its waters first begin to mingle with those of the Columbia at the southern end of Sauvie Island.

The Multnomah tribe of the Chinook occupied this island for centuries, trading both upriver and downriver. Eventually a few white explorers came and went. Lewis and Clark stopped long enough to map the island as Wappatoo, after a tuber that grew abundantly there and formed a significant part of the local diet, but Portlanders now call this fifteen-mile-long island Sauvie *(So-Vee)*, a mispronunciation of the surname of Laurent Sauvé, a white manager for a branch of the Hudson Bay Company. Some even call it Sauvie's Island, as if this fellow once owned the whole 24,000 acres, but in fact Sauvé only oversaw a dairy herd and performed other administrative duties on the island for the company in the early 1800s. He didn't even live out his full life there but retired at the age of fifty-five and moved to Canada. The names that would have made the most sense to the island's history, culture, and predominant food source didn't stick, at least not with the white population that settled the island and the nearby city.

Where the waters of the two rivers meet is called Kelly Point. The Willamette continues on one side, the side where I live, in the form of a quiet, curving, narrow channel; the great, wide Columbia charges along on the other side. At the northernmost point of the island is Warrior Point, and here waters of the Willamette end when the Multnomah Channel flows into the Columbia and the river heads on toward Astoria.

For many years, my three dogs (Carson, Boon, and Brio respectively) and I walked the island together or with neighbors and various friends. My neighbor Salli and I wore out several pairs of shoes walking Boon every day of the first ten years of his life on a three-mile trail around a shallow lake. My neighbor Julia and I often took Brio on the same trail.

Brio was a cattle dog/whippet mix who had been found on the streets of Bakersfield with her two puppies. All three were living a dangerous and hardscrabble life, and all three were caught

Upriver.

and transferred from Kern County to the Los Angeles County Animal Control's death row. A rescue group swept up the mother and pups on the morning of the day they were to be killed and found homes for them.

Carson had been raised in the city but near big parks with lots of running room, and then she spent the majority of her life on the houseboat with its nearby forest and trails, along with plenty of beach time. Boon had spent almost his entire life here. Both took the natural world, especially the island with its trail just downriver from us, as a given.

But the green of Oregon thrilled and astonished Brio each and every day in a way I'd never witnessed in a dog. She might have been

Bakersfield street smart, but a world of forest and flowing water was Oz to her. Each morning she sniffed eagerly at the parking lot with its landscape of trees and flowers planted by our beloved neighbor Kevin before he died. If at any point during the day I opened the door so she could lie on the swim float and watch the birds and smell the river, she paused on her way out to look up at me with a gratitude that melted my heart.

On one walk not long after I brought her home from the rescue agency in California, it was not only Brio, but Julia and I who were astounded when, as she loped alongside us, panting and happy, a small bird flew into, and then immediately out of, her mouth. Her shocked eyes questioned us: *Did you see that? How often does this sort of thing happen?* We had to admit to her that it was probably a once-in-a-lifetime experience; then again, who could

Downriver.

64

say? She'd been freed from death row at the eleventh hour. Anything could happen.

I've mentioned that this long and narrow island is a bird sanctuary, but hunters gather to shoot geese and ducks during hunting seasons. Of course the gunfire alarms large flocks of birds, and they rise, terrified, and fill the sky, heading upriver, downriver, and in all directions, finally settling down somewhere else. Farmers' markets, nurseries, horse stables, small farms, a school, and land set aside for hiking comprise the human administered activity on the island, but wildness is ever present. Julia and I once saw a cougar hunting for ducks on Virginia Lake. Brio missed it because she was too short to see over the tall grass along the lake's edge. We retreated and headed back toward the parking lot, but on our way, we ran into a woman we'd met on the trail many times. Patty was around eighty and a long-term resident of one of the island's houseboat moorages downriver from ours. We told her about the cougar. She wanted to know where and hurried off in the direction I pointed, calling over her shoulder that she planned to go around to the other side of the lake in hopes of getting a better look. Not long after that, I saw her again as I drove down Sauvie Island Road to get some flowers at the farmers' market. She was retrieving her mail and cheerily waved at me, so if an encounter happened, it must have gone well.

Deer sometimes swim from the mainland to the island and vice versa. One morning Julia spotted four deer swimming downriver in the middle of the channel and then climbing onto the mainland just past the end of the moorage.

There's a famous nude beach on the Columbia River side. A book I love that tells what the island is like in terms of its place in nature and echoes from its past is *Nude Beach Notebook*, a memoir by my friend Barbara Scot, a houseboat resident there.

Because it's gently rolling and sometimes flat with a far horizon, the island does remind me of the Midwest, just as friends had told me it would when I first moved here. Bicyclists love it for this reason, and I spent a summer bicycling around it long ago. But I prefer to walk it, to lose myself in the moss-covered oaks, the bird sounds and sightings, and the old trails where my dogs once ran with joy. Eventually I remember to find my car again, drive upriver on the narrow road along the dyke, and cross the bridge to home.

PART THREE

Full Circle

When I was a child, I lived in several small towns across the Midwest: North Dakota, South Dakota, Minnesota, Wisconsin, Iowa. My father was busy climbing the ladder of responsibility in a chain of far-flung department stores— shoe salesman to shoe department assistant manager to shoe department manager to first-floor assistant manager, etc. Each new position required a transfer to another town, meaning not only he but my mother, my two older brothers, my younger sister, and I faced constant change. The moment we settled in to new friendships in our classrooms and neighborhood, the moving van pulled up and we had to wave goodbye. I learned to hold fast to good memories, sometimes going over everything that had happened so far, trying hard to conjure a mental picture of everyone I'd ever known, determined not to forget them.

When I was ten, I bought a used bicycle with allowance money I'd saved. My fantasy was to leave home for a summer at fifteen, an age at which it seemed to me anything would be possible. My idea was to ride my bike back through my life, visiting friends in all the towns we'd ever lived. But when I turned fifteen at last, my parents quickly vetoed this idea as too dangerous.

Soon we moved again, and I entered a new high school as a junior, an awkward time within the most awkward set of years. Once again I was surrounded by people who'd known one another since kindergarten. In my shyness and extreme social discomfort, I replaced my old fantasy with another: one day I'd live in a small village and ride my bike up and down a single, long street of houses and shops where I could stop and say hello to anybody there because I'd know them all well.

I can still see the images I created in my mind as a young girl. The street, eternally sunny, stretched out before me, each structure unique and three dimensional but the same soft sand tone in color, as if all were made of the same material. Combining difference with sameness seemed to be an important element of this vision. As I rode along on my bike, people spoke to me from windows and doorways, their faces familiar and friendly. Living in a community where I knew everyone and could be known by them became my secret dream. I turned to it over and over again for comfort.

And then I grew up. Through the years I only recalled this vision sporadically as I moved from place to place, unconsciously replicating what had been forced upon me when a child. In the span of only ten years or so, I lived in two college towns, Ames and Iowa City, followed by a year in the Middle East, and then on to Vancouver, British Columbia; Portland, Oregon; Boston; Seattle; back to the outskirts of Portland; and then three apartments within the city. Finally, in my mid-thirties, I arrived at the moorage.

One day not long ago as I was walking down the dock, I saw Salli out watering her floating garden, a large wooden deck in the backwater

that she'd tied to the walkway. I told her about finding a pair of chipmunks deep in the container of birdseed I kept on my deck. They'd been stuffing themselves and lumbered off, heavy as stones, in the direction of the ramp and back to the hard life of the forest. Salli assured me they wouldn't stay there. She'd seen them dashing from houseboat to houseboat, looking for more birdseed and other easy food.

I walked on and met up with Melissa loaded down with books and bags stuffed with papers, returning home from a day of teaching high school Spanish. Yes, she'd seen the chipmunks too and had heard they'd even dashed into Julia's house, but the cats chased them right back out. Farther along, Joan joined me, tapping her Fitbit and announcing how many more steps she needed to reach her goal of 12,000 for the day. We ran into Burt paddling his kayak along the backwater, heading to

Turtle in the backwater.

the ramp where he'd haul the kayak up to his car and set off to paddle with friends near Clatskanie.

Half an hour later, after a few more neighborly encounters and after Joan met her exercise goal and returned home to set up a field camera to film some otters who'd been visiting her deck every night, I was walking home alone in the twilight when my old vision for myself suddenly came back after a long, long absence. I experienced one of those moments when all the connections are made somewhere outside of time and then yanked back into time to stand plainly before you, leaving you with a sense of inevitability. For a few seconds, the walkway seemed to undulate ahead of me. No wonder I'd had a premonition when I'd first driven past this moorage all those years ago and my head turned, without my willing it, toward the string of houses off in the distance—all so different from one another and yet all the same: houseboats. No wonder I felt something calling to me: *Look This Way. You Are Here.*

Too bad about that perpetually sunny part missing, but then this is Oregon.

Goslings.

Houseboat

After all these years of living on it
I am becoming the river
My mind moves more and more like water
turned blue and green and silver by reflection
Water moving, moving all the time
Moving even as I sleep

Sometimes in the company of others
I can't understand their words
Their words float over me like bird calls
I am ripples, light and shadow
Trees fall across my face

Late nights lying alone I wonder
To what ocean are my thoughts returning
even now?
In the cool foggy morning I wonder
To what ocean will my thoughts return
When I am gone?
"The cat needs her breakfast."
"Where did I put the keys?"
"I've been sitting here—staring—a long time, I suppose."

Outside, six plump geese guard nests
When they see me at the window they cry out
Six rusty gates opening at once

If I watch them long enough
If I am still enough, plump enough
They take me in
The scolding stops
Quiet seeps through windows, floorboards
the soles of my feet
And rises, rises
Filling my legs and pelvis
Filling belly, heart, lungs
Filling my wings, my goosey throat, my feathers, my feathertips

Quiet dissolves me
Liquid, I fill the silent house

— Andrea Carlisle

Looking Downriver, Island Side (1990s).

Acknowledgements

For her organizational expertise, dependable reassurance, a willingness to remain calm while falling into whirlpools of information to help me fine tune and sort through how this book could meet a public, and for the many long hours she spent helping get it ready for printing as well as for her tasteful and tactful suggestions along the way, I'm indebted to Meg Glaser.

To Joanne Mulcahy, for her friendship and editorial advice in this writing endeavor and in so many others, I give my heartfelt thanks. What a lucky day when we bonded over a kettle of steaming broccoli all those years ago at the Oregon Writers' Colony. Everlasting gratitude to Teresa Jordan for knowing we'd be friends and bringing us together and for her friendship and faithful encouragement.

Michael and Petra Mathers blew hard on the spark that became the impetus to make sure this book happened. Petra's reading of its earliest pages cheered me on and Michael's help along the way with photographs was invaluable. His gift of a camera provided the key to making this book come together and has helped me see my familiar moorage in new ways.

Many thanks to other friends whose encouragement kept my internal river of ideas and inspiration flowing: Bob Hazen, Katharine and Alan Cahn, Leigh Coffey, Judy Teufel, Thalia Zepatos, Esther Podemski, Diane McDevitt, Scott Lyons, Ketzel Levine, Justin Ting, Kathryn Hunt, Joan Gratz, Julia Helfritz, Kathy Moriarty, Claudia Johnson, and Susan Walsh. Thanks, pals! And I appreciate, too, all the Facebook friends who receive every photo and story of the river I share there with a warm welcome.

Warm thanks to Kristen Hall-Geisler and Cooper Lee Bombardier at Indigo for their fine-tooth-word combs, which they handle with such skill, and to Sarah Klinger for both her design and research skills.

I so appreciate my friend and neighbor Salli's generosity in loaning her paintings of the moorage and the river to this project, as well as for her thoughtful reading of the text in draft form.

If you'd like to see more photographs of the moorage and river, follow @carlisle7434 on Instagram. See andreacarlisle.com for more about the author.

Special thanks to Aunt Mattie, my model
for finding a little house in a place you love
and staying put.

Made in the USA
Columbia, SC
15 May 2020